WHAT WE DEMAND

1. Comprehensive and effective *civil rights legislation* from the present Congress—without compromise or filibuster—to guarantee all Americans
   - access to all public accommodations
   - decent housing
   - adequate and integrated education
   - the right to vote

2. Withholding of Federal funds from all programs in which discrimination exists.

3. *Desegregation of all school districts in 1963.*

4. Enforcement of the *Fourteenth Amendment*—reducing Congressional representation of states where citizens are disfranchised.

5. A new *Executive Order* banning discrimination in all housing supported by federal funds.

6. Authority for the Attorney General to institute *injunctive suits* when any constitutional right is violated.

7. A massive federal program to train and place all unemployed workers—Negro and white—on meaningful and dignified jobs at decent wages.

8. A national *minimum wage* act that will give all Americans a decent standard of living. (Government surveys show that anything less than $2.00 an hour fails to do this.)

9. A broadened *Fair Labor Standards* Act to include all areas of employment which are presently excluded.

10. A federal *Fair Employment Practices* Act barring discrimination by federal, state, and municipal governments, and by employers, contractors, employment agencies, and trade unions.

To all young people who
protest for peace and justice
—MGL

To Juanita, thank you for being such a positive force in my life.
Thank you for our talks that have educated me and inspired me to
learn more about Black history. You taught me how to be proud of
who I am, where I come from, and to do so with grace and integrity.
You are, and always have been, an example of Black excellence in
my eyes, and the impact you've had on my life is immeasurable.
Thank you.
—BJ

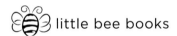 little bee books

New York, NY
Text copyright © 2023 by Michael G. Long
Illustrations copyright © 2023 by Bea Jackson
Manufactured in China   RRD 0123
First Edition
10 9 8 7 6 5 4 3 2 1

Library of Congress Cataloging-in-Publication Data is available upon request.
ISBN 978-1-4998-1206-0
littlebeebooks.com
For information about special discounts on bulk purchases,
please contact Little Bee Books at sales@littlebeebooks.com.

About the type:
The cover and title page are set in Bayard, a typeface designed by Tré Seals and inspired by the iconic signs carried during the 1963 March on Washington for Jobs and Freedom. It was named after Bayard Rustin, the subject of this book, and organizer of this historic event.

WRITTEN BY **MICHAEL G. LONG**   ILLUSTRATED BY **BEA JACKSON**

UNSTOPPABLE

HOW BAYARD RUSTIN ORGANIZED THE 1963 MARCH ON WASHINGTON

Bayard Rustin was a troublemaker.

Bayard grew up in West Chester, Pennsylvania, where white business owners and city officials wanted to separate Black and white people in places like elementary schools, restaurants, and movie theaters. But Bayard didn't care. In high school, he sat in the white section of the town's main movie theater. The police arrested him even though there were no laws requiring segregation.

A few years later, he was arrested again,
this time for sitting next to white people on a bus.

Bayard was making trouble for a good reason:
he wanted to change the laws and customs
that kept Black people from living freely.

Bayard wasn't the only one challenging unjust laws. As an adult, Bayard lived in New York City near his mentor, A. Philip Randolph, who had long fought for the rights of Black workers. Throughout the 1940s and '50s, they shared their dreams of freedom.

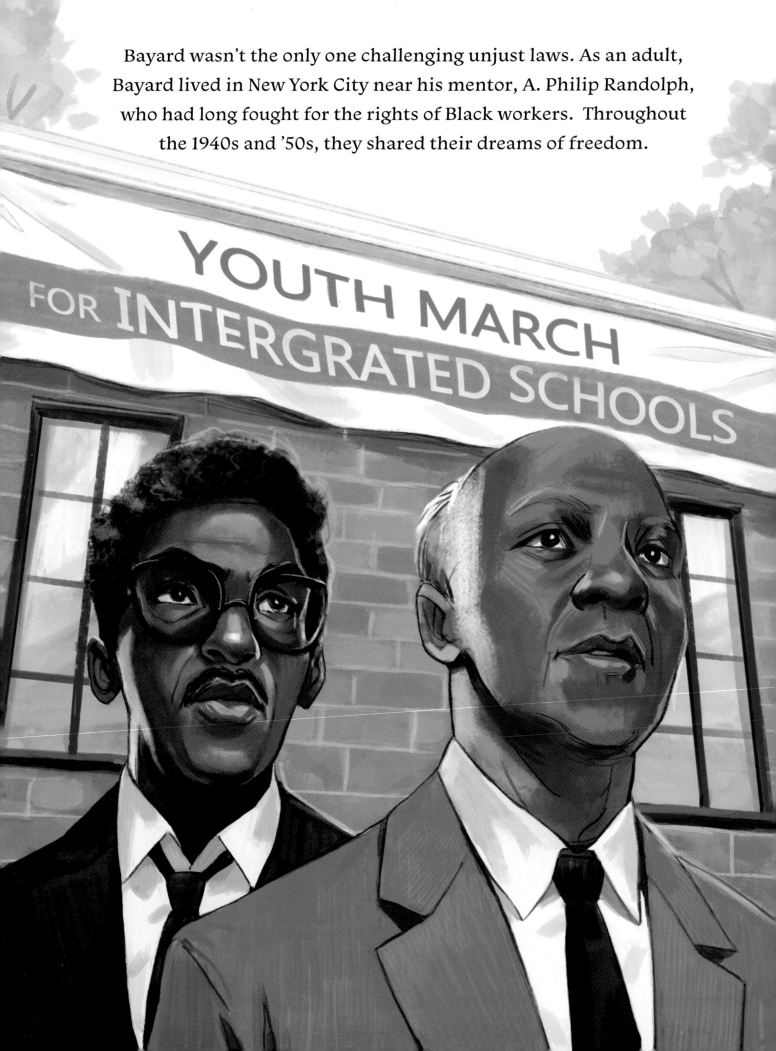

They dreamed of schools where Black and white children could learn together.

They dreamed of good, safe jobs that paid well.

They dreamed of decent homes and being treated with respect and dignity.

But there were powerful people and forces determined to keep their dreams from coming true. So Bayard and Mr. Randolph would have to fight.

Bayard was a peaceful man. How could he fight without being violent? And how could he make enough trouble to shake the whole nation?

Bayard was inspired by a man named Mohandas Gandhi, also a troublemaker fighting for freedom. Gandhi took on the entire British empire, using rallies, strikes, and marches to free India from British rule.

His most famous protest was a massive march to the Indian Ocean that received worldwide attention. This march inspired people across the globe to protest for their own rights.

We can march, too! Bayard thought.

In 1962, Mr. Randolph and Bayard imagined the largest march for civil rights that the United States had ever seen. Bayard had already organized many protests against war, nuclear weapons, racial segregation in public schools, and racial discrimination in businesses.

Now, he would lead a civil rights protest to the doorstep of the United States government.

Bayard and Mr. Randolph called it the
March on Washington for Jobs and Freedom.

The march would demand that politicians end discrimination by passing laws without delay. They wanted immediate action that could be felt everywhere in the country. If it worked, the march would be a massive victory for the civil rights movement.

It was a great plan, but Bayard faced a big challenge. . . .

Powerful people and forces who did not want Black equality threatened to destroy the movement. Some white politicians attacked Bayard for many things, including for being gay.

Bayard was living in a time when it was illegal to live and love as he pleased. Some civil rights leaders worried the attacks on Bayard would harm the fight for Black freedom. They didn't want him to be part of the fight. But Bayard was proud of who he was—Black, gay, and an activist for peace.

Bayard feared his dream was over.

Other movement leaders, including future congressman
John Lewis and Martin Luther King Jr., strongly disagreed.

They admired Bayard and believed his planning skills were too valuable to lose. They made sure Bayard was the main organizer of the march.

There was no time to celebrate.
The March on Washington for Jobs and Freedom
was only eight weeks away!

Bayard and his staff of over 200 volunteers got to work.
They called newspaper offices, television stations,
families and schools, churches and synagogues,
labor unions and community groups.

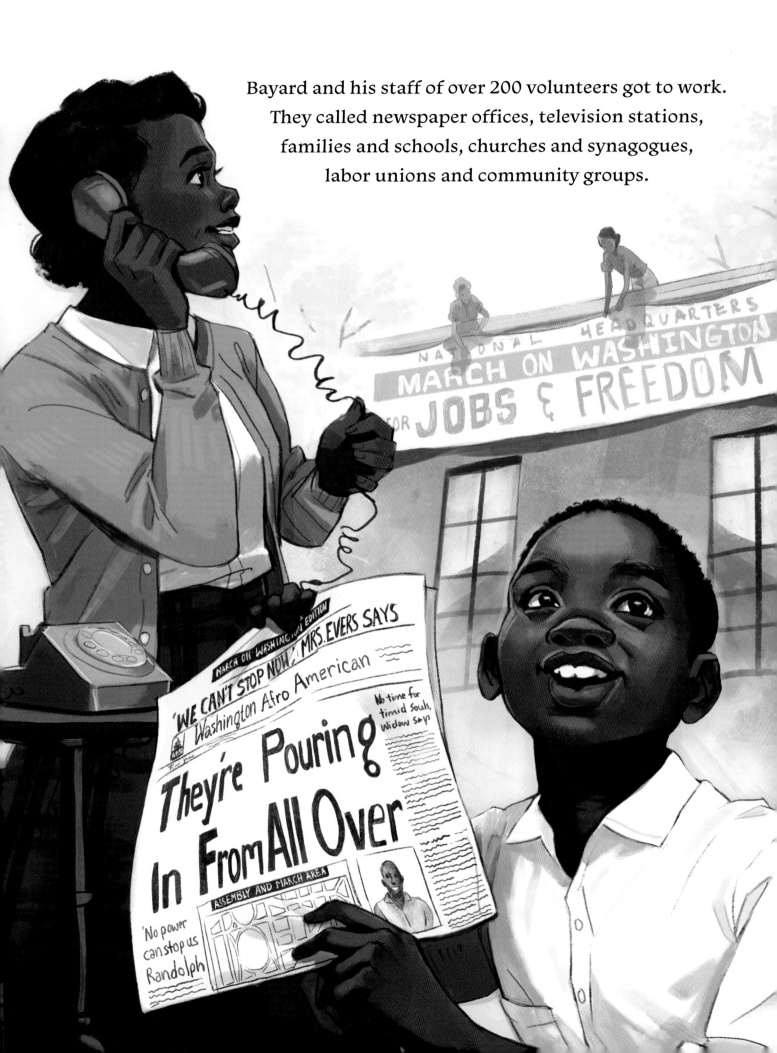

They organized travel on buses, trains, and planes to bring people from all over the country.

They built first aid stations,
made lunches,
and even rented two hundred portable toilets!

No detail escaped Bayard's attention.

One of Bayard's main goals was to educate protestors about nonviolent fighting. Black protesters in the United States had faced horrible violence. Bayard wanted everyone to be prepared for the worst— and he didn't want them to hit back.

Instead of making fists, they could hold signs about freedom.
Instead of kicking, they should walk from
the Washington Monument to the Lincoln Memorial.
Instead of shouting ugly names, they would sing beautiful songs.

On August 28th, 1963, Bayard woke up early and walked to the Washington Monument. Only a few hundred marchers had arrived. Bayard was scared that people might not come.

His worries soon disappeared.
By 9:30 a.m., 40,000 people were ready to march.

Then there were 90,000.

The protestors kept coming. The excitement kept building.

By the time the march began,
about 250,000 people had arrived!

They wanted to vote with their footsteps and raise their voices so loud that the president himself would have to answer.

And with these brave protestors,
Dr. King shared his dream for freedom.

At the end of the day, Bayard and Mr. Randolph took a moment to reflect on all that had happened. They knew the fight was not over, but the March on Washington marked a bold new step toward justice. Their protest shook the nation, and in the coming years, powerful people and forces would pass laws that were right and fair.

Bayard Rustin was a troublemaker— and his dream of change had finally come true.

AUTHOR'S NOTE

Born on March 17, 1912, Bayard Rustin was raised by his grandparents, Julia and Janifer Rustin, in West Chester, Pennsylvania. Julia taught him the Quaker belief that every person has equal worth and dignity.

Bayard detested the unfair treatment he received because of the color of his skin and developed a reputation for resisting discrimination.

As a pacifist, Bayard opposed World War II and refused to be drafted as a soldier. The government arrested him in 1944, and he spent two years in federal prison for refusing to fight. Following his release in 1946, Bayard organized the Journey of Reconciliation, a protest designed to desegregate buses in the South.

In the early 1950s, Bayard traveled the country, giving lectures on the dangers of nuclear weapons, and embracing world peace. While in California in 1953, he was arrested for engaging in homosexual behavior.

Two years later, Bayard traveled to Montgomery, Alabama, to help Martin Luther King, Jr. lead a bus boycott protesting segregated seating. Bayard taught King about using nonviolent tactics and accepting pacifism as a way of life.

Bayard advised King on civil rights for the next two decades. Perhaps most helpful was Bayard's plan to build a new organization that would use nonviolent campaigns for racial justice throughout the South.

Bayard and labor leader A. Phillip Randolph teamed up in the late 1950s when they brought thousands of young people to Washington, DC, for marches demanding the immediate integration of public schools. Then in 1963, the pair began calling for the March on Washington for Jobs and Freedom. Civil rights leaders asked Bayard to plan the entire event in just eight weeks.

On August 28, 1963, about 250,000 people attended the march and heard Dr. King share his dream that Black and white children would one day be free to live and play together. The massive crowd also cheered Bayard as he demanded that Black people receive good jobs and equal justice under the law. The march was the largest demonstration for civil rights up to that point in history, and it led to laws advancing civil rights for Black Americans.

For Bayard, the march didn't end until he and a group of five hundred volunteers cleaned the entire route, making sure no cup, scrap of paper, or piece of litter remained. He wanted to make sure no one could accuse the protest of being disorderly.

After the march, Bayard continued to fight for human rights across the globe. And with the encouragement of his partner, Walter Naegle, Bayard publicly supported gay and lesbian rights.

President Barack Obama awarded Bayard the Presidential Medal of Freedom posthumously on November 20, 2013. Naegle accepted the award in a White House ceremony. When speaking of Bayard, President Obama said, "For decades, this great leader, often at Dr. King's side, was denied his rightful place in history because he was openly gay. No medal can change that, but today, we honor Bayard Rustin's memory by taking our place in his march toward true equality, no matter who we are or who we love."

MY RESEARCH

While researching Bayard and his history-changing accomplishments, I contacted his partner, Walter Naegle. More than anything else, my conversations with Naegle, and then with Bayard's friends and colleagues, helped me understand his character—his true thoughts and inner feelings.

After I spoke with Naegle, I visited the Library of Congress in Washington, DC, where many of Bayard's papers—his letters, speeches, articles, and interviews—are located. I also visited other places that held his writings, including the National Archives in College Park, Maryland. At the same time, I looked for references to Bayard in many newspaper and magazine articles, especially those written while he was still alive and active in the peace and civil rights movements.

History books also became very important to my work. Two stand out in particular: John D'Emilio's *Lost Prophet: The Life and Times of Bayard Rustin* and *Time on Two Crosses: The Collected Writings of Bayard Rustin*, edited by Devon Carbado and Don Weise. For young readers, I recommend a book that I coauthored with Walter Naegle and Jacqueline Houtman—*Troublemaker for Justice: The Story of Bayard Rustin, the Man Behind the March on Washington*. For everyone, I suggest watching Nancy Kates's and Bennet Singer's powerful documentary titled *Brother Outsider: The Life of Bayard Rustin*.